My Little Book of
Life Cycles

by Camilla de la Bédoyère

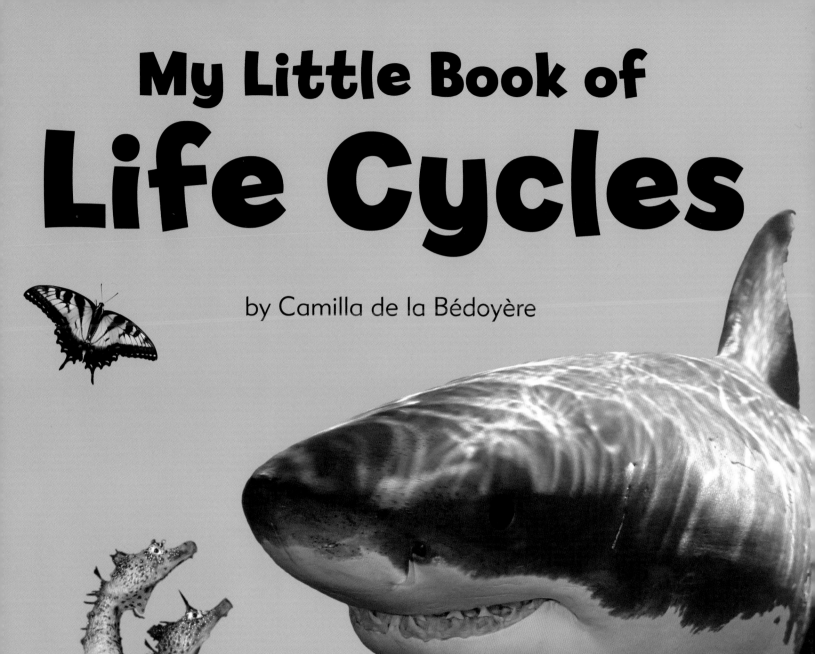

QED Publishing

Copyright © QED Publishing 2014

Designer: Andrew Crowson
Editor: Ruth Symons

First published in the UK in 2014 by
QED Publishing
A Quarto Group company
The Old Brewery
6 Blundell Street
London N7 9BH

www.qed-publishing.co.uk

A catalogue record for this book is available
from the British Library.

ISBN 978 1 78171 554 3

Printed in China

Words in **bold** are explained in the glossary on page 60.

Contents

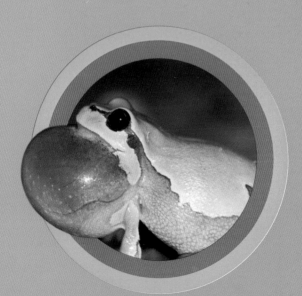

What is a life cycle?

The way that animals begin life, grow and have babies is called a life cycle.

When an animal begins its life we say it has hatched, or has been born.

Young animals eat, grow and explore the world. When they have grown bigger they become adults.

6

⌃ **Adult butterfly**

5

≪ **Butterfly crawls out of pupa**

The life cycle of a butterfly has many stages.

4

≪ **Pupa forms around caterpillar**

⌄ **Caterpillar**

3

7

>> Baby animals often have special names. Baby kangaroos are called joeys.

^ **Butterfly ready to lay eggs**

8

ˇ When animals become adults they can have their own babies.

>> **Butterfly dies at end of life cycle**

>> **Eggs**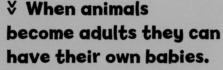

1

<< **Newly hatched caterpillar**

2

The story of a frog

⌄ In spring, male and female frogs come together to mate. They always mate in water.

A frog is an **amphibian**. It spends part of its life in water, and part of its life on land.

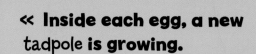

« Inside each egg, a new tadpole **is growing**.

Amphibians lay their eggs in water.
As the female lays her eggs, the
male covers them with a liquid, which
fertilizes them. The eggs stick together
in a big clump called frogspawn.

>> **After a few weeks,
the eggs hatch.**

Tiny tadpoles

Tadpoles are tiny when they hatch, but they quickly grow.

Each tadpole has a long tail, which it uses to swim. It has feathery **gills** on either side of its head. These allow the young tadpole to breathe underwater.

⌃ **A frog spends the first two stages of its life cycle in the water.**

To begin with, tadpoles just eat small water plants. Later, they will also eat pond animals.

« Tadpoles grow faster when they live in warm water with plenty of food.

9

The big change

When they are about seven weeks old, tadpoles begin to change into frogs.

First, they grow back legs. A few weeks later, their gills disappear. Then they swim to the surface to breathe air. Their tails begin to shrink and their front legs grow.

3

1

2

ᐱ As its legs grow longer, the tail grows shorter.

ᐱ The tadpole's back legs grow first.

ᐱ Then its front legs begin to grow.

4

⋎ By the time it is 12 weeks old, the tiny frog is about 3 centimetres long.

≪ The little frogs keep growing, and their tails disappear. They are now called froglets.

Adult life

Adult frogs spend most of their time on land. They hunt for insects, slugs and worms.

⩔ **Frogs are ready to mate when they are two to three years old.**

≫ **Frogs** hibernate **in the winter, when there is little food to eat, and the weather is cold.**

>> Male tree frogs croak loudly to call the females to mate.

In spring, frogs return to the pond where they were born. This is where the adult frogs mate. Soon the story of the life cycle will begin again.

The story of a butterfly

A butterfly is a type of **insect**. Insects have three pairs of legs, making six legs altogether.

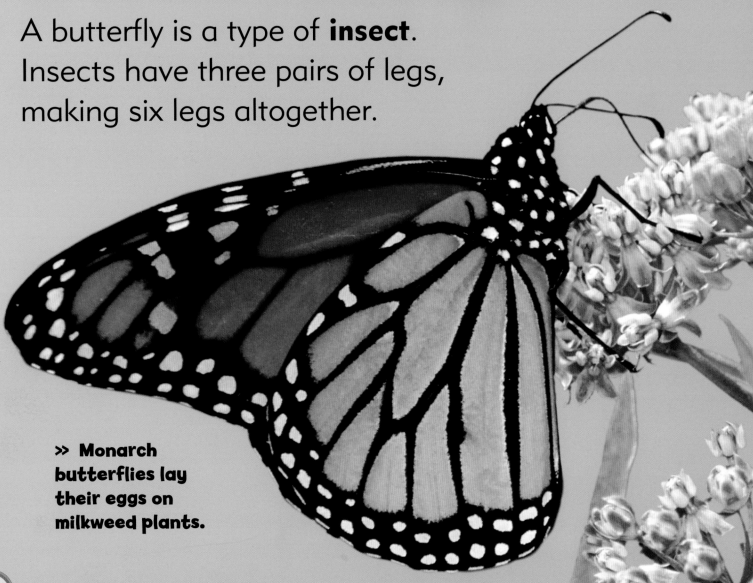

>> **Monarch butterflies lay their eggs on milkweed plants.**

In spring, a female butterfly searches for somewhere safe to lay her eggs. She lays them under leaves. The eggs stick to the leaves and are hidden from view.

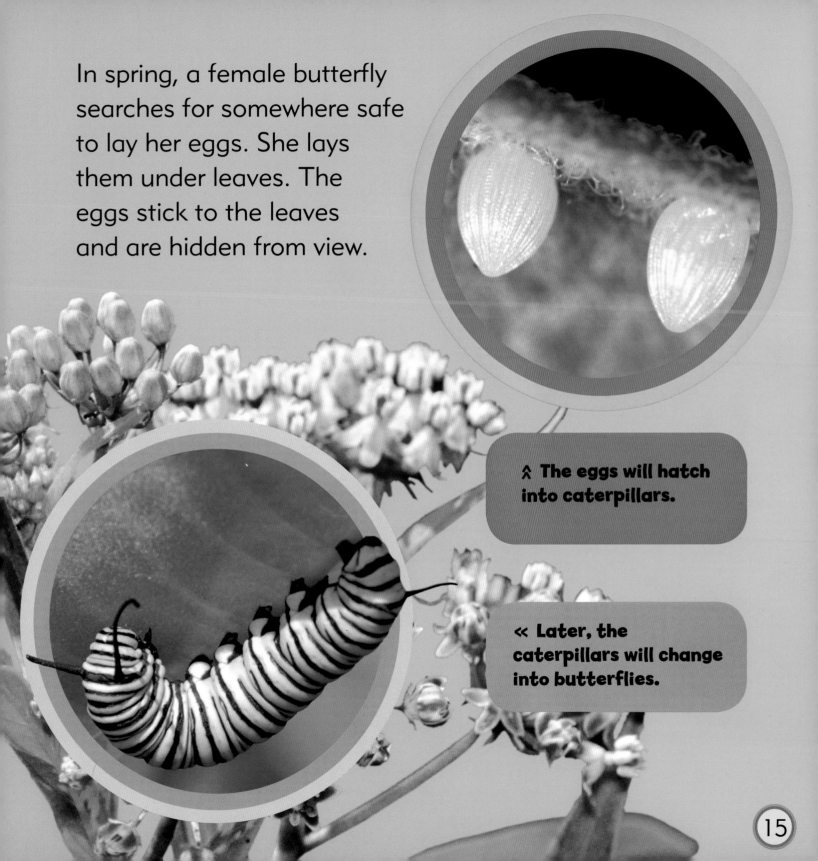

ꙮ The eggs will hatch into caterpillars.

« Later, the caterpillars will change into butterflies.

The eggs hatch

A few days later, the eggs hatch, and a tiny yellow caterpillar comes out of each one.

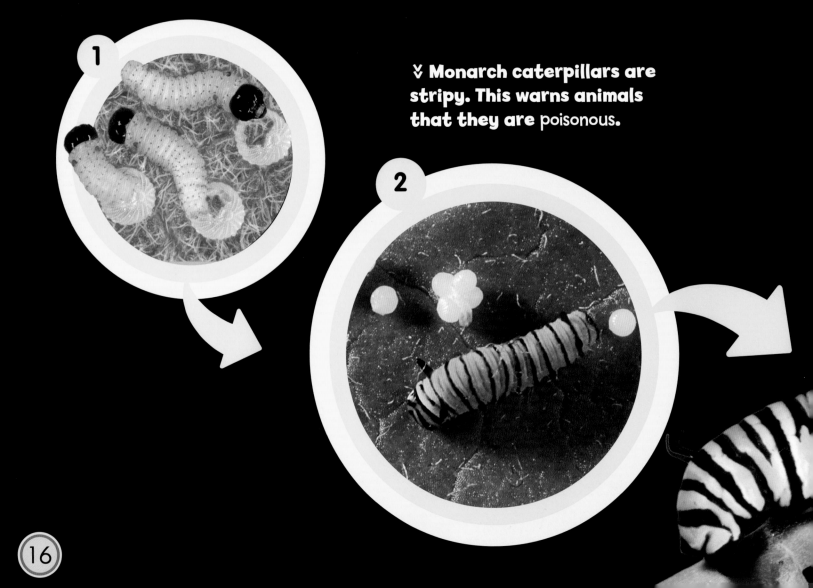

1

2

⌄ **Monarch caterpillars are stripy. This warns animals that they are** poisonous.

As a caterpillar grows, its skin becomes too tight, and splits. The caterpillar sheds its skin, revealing a new one underneath. This is called **moulting**.

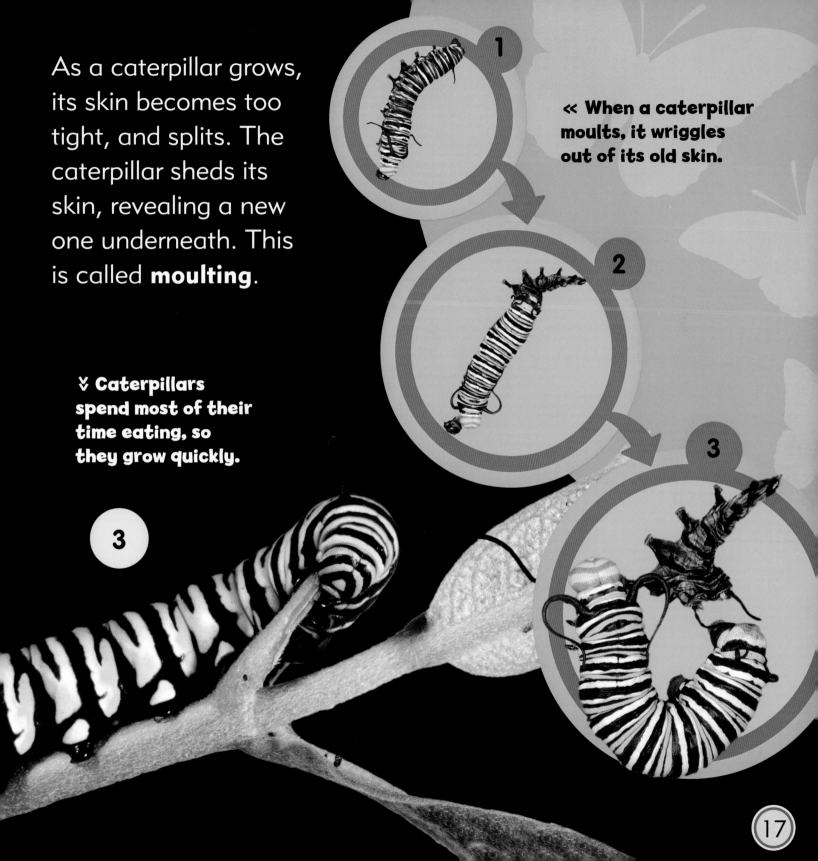

1

« **When a caterpillar moults, it wriggles out of its old skin.**

2

3

∀ **Caterpillars spend most of their time eating, so they grow quickly.**

3

Transformation

After about 14 days, a caterpillar is ready to change into a **pupa**. This is the next stage of its life cycle.

1

2

Pupa

« The caterpillar makes a silk thread, and uses it to hang from a leaf.

A caterpillar moults one last time, then it turns into a pupa. Inside the pupa, the caterpillar gradually changes. After about two weeks, the pupa cracks open and the butterfly crawls out.

⌄ **The butterfly spreads its wings so they can dry.**

3

4

⌃ **The butterfly has to rest for a few hours before it can fly.**

A long journey

As the summer comes to an end, monarch butterflies start an amazing journey, called a **migration**.

« Millions of monarch butterflies spend the winter resting on trees.

The monarch butterflies wake up when warm weather arrives.

They fly to warmer places.
The journey can cover thousands
of miles and takes more than two
months. In spring, the butterflies
set off to their summer homes.
On the way, they mate.

>> Male and female
monarchs look similar,
but males have small dark
spots on their back wings.

The story of a penguin

Emperor penguins live in big groups called **colonies**. Their home is in the Antarctic, which is at the bottom of our planet Earth.

>> **Males and females call each other. The sound they make is called a bray.**

At the start of winter, emperor penguins meet on sheets of ice to mate. A male mates with a female and fertilizes the egg inside her body.

>> After mating, the male and female stay together.

⋏ An egg has to be fertilized before it can grow into a chick.

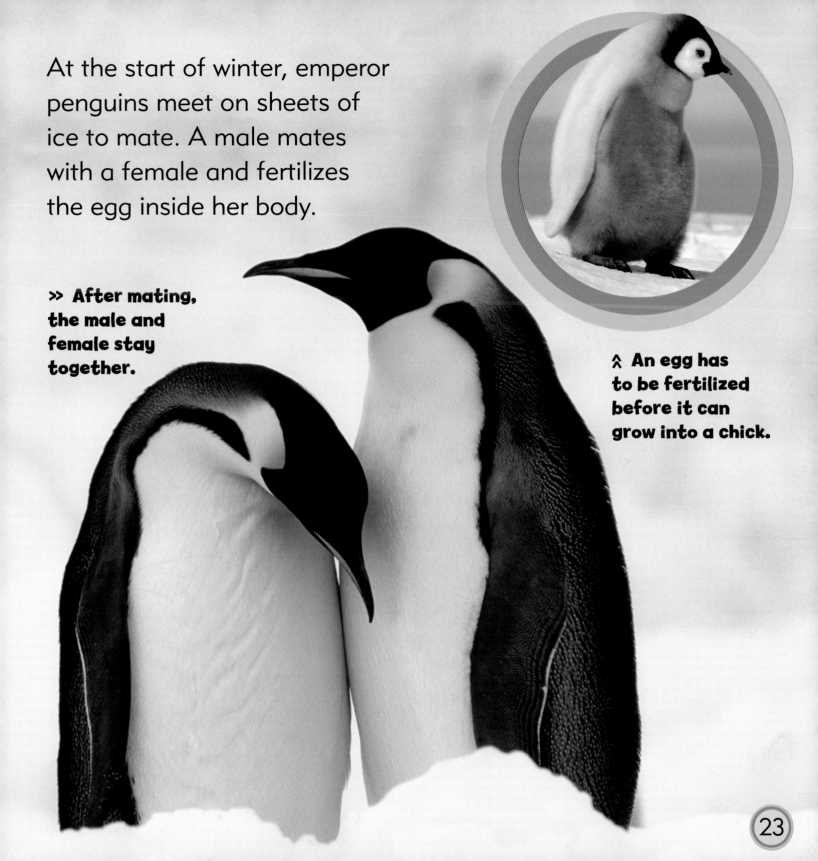

Laying an egg

Emperor penguins do not build nests. They carry their eggs instead.

The female lays a single egg. The male uses his beak to push it onto his feet. He has a bare patch of skin on his belly, called a brood patch. He lays this over the egg.

2

1

« **The egg has a strong shell on the outside.**

⌃ **The brood patch keeps the egg warm.**

The egg is on the male's feet, where it will be kept warm.

3

Gentoo penguins build a nest for their eggs.

The long walk

The males look after the eggs and the females walk back to the sea. The long walk takes four weeks.

>> **The female penguins catch lots of fish and fill their stomachs with food.**

<< **The males do not eat while the females are away. They huddle together to keep warm.**

After feeding, the female walks back to the colony and finds her mate. Now the male can give the egg to the mother. He walks to the sea to find food.

« The female takes her egg from the male.

The egg hatches

The chick breaks out of the shell. It sits on its mother's feet to keep warm.

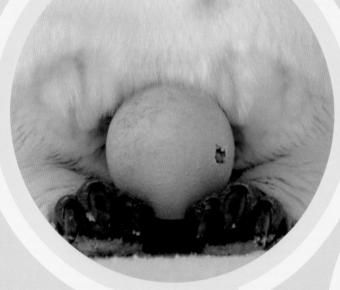

1

⌃ **The shell begins to crack open.**

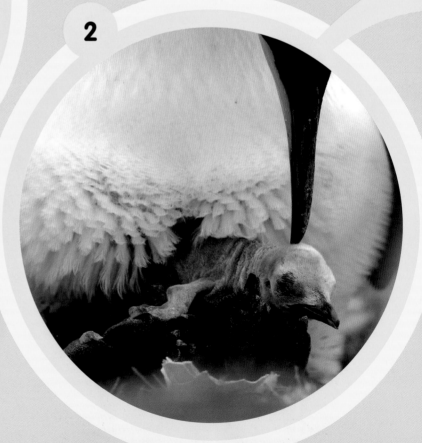

2

≫ **The chick comes out of the shell.**

The father comes back from the sea. He has a stomach full of food. The parents take it in turns to feed the chick. They keep it warm and safe.

3

** The parents feed the chick with food from their stomach.

>> The chick stays with its parents.

Chicks together

When the chicks are seven weeks old they huddle together. A group of chicks is called a crèche.

⌃ **Adult penguins take it in turns to look after the crèche.**

As they grow, the chicks get new feathers. Soon they will look like their parents. When they are adults, the young penguins will find mates. The life cycle will begin again.

>> Chicks lose their fluffy feathers as new feathers start growing.

>> Young penguins know how to swim. Their parents do not have to teach them.

The story of a sea horse

A sea horse is a type of fish. It has **scales**, a tail and **fins**.

Fins

Tail

>> Male sea horses choose the biggest females to mate with.

<< Sea horses have a long tail and tiny fins.

Before they mate, male and female sea horses dance for each other. Their special mating dance is part of **courtship**. The sea horses wrap their tails around each other, and swim together.

⌄ **A baby sea horse is called a fry.**

Life begins

A male sea horse has a special pouch on his belly. After dancing, the pouch gets bigger.

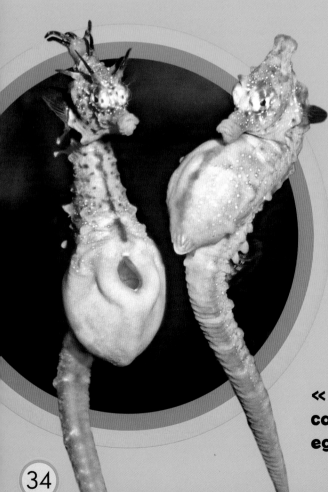

⌄ The male and female stay close together so that no eggs are lost.

≪ The female carefully passes her eggs to the male.

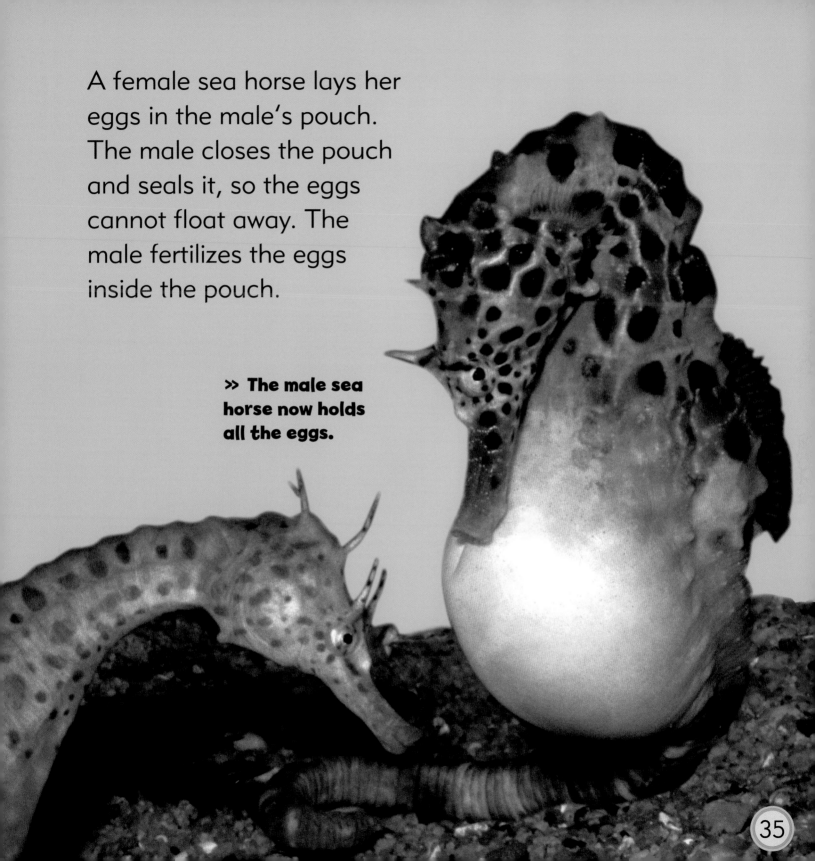

A female sea horse lays her eggs in the male's pouch. The male closes the pouch and seals it, so the eggs cannot float away. The male fertilizes the eggs inside the pouch.

>> The male sea horse now holds all the eggs.

Caring for the eggs

The fertilized eggs stay in the male sea horse's pouch for up to six weeks.

>> The pouches of these two pregnant males are filled with tiny fry.

Each egg has food for the fry growing inside it. Some fry also get food from their father's body. As soon as the fry are born they swim away.

⌃ **The male pushes the fry out from his pouch quickly.**

>> **The fry are too small to swim well. They wrap their tails around plants or coral.**

Growing up

The hatchlings are very small when they are born. As they get older they grow bigger.

>> This is a zebra-snout sea horse. It will be an adult when it is nine months old.

<< Fry eat small sea animals such as brine shrimp.

Sea horses suck up food through their snout.

The fry have to look after themselves, as their parents do not look after them. Fry have to find food, and will need to hide from bigger fish who will try to eat them.

The story of a shark

A shark is a kind of fish. Young sharks are called pups. All pups begin life as eggs.

⌄ **Sharks are excellent swimmers. Their fins help them to swim and to change direction.**

Before a female shark can have pups, she must mate with a male shark. The male grabs the female with special fins called claspers. He may even bite the female.

« **The male fertilizes the female's eggs. Only fertilized eggs can grow into new sharks.**

>> Only male sharks have fins called claspers.

Giving birth

Some sharks lay their eggs on the seabed before they hatch. The pups of some sharks grow inside their mother until they are born.

>> **This newborn pup is still attached to its placenta.**

≪ As soon as the pups are born, the mother swims away. The pups have to survive by themselves.

⌄ A great white shark mother's eggs hatch inside her. The first pups to hatch eat the other eggs.

The pups of lemon sharks grow from eggs inside their mother's body. Before hatching, the pups get food through the **placenta**. After about a year, the pups are born.

Laying eggs

Female swell sharks must find a safe place to lay their eggs.

Each egg is held in a rubbery case called a mermaid's purse. It has long strings called tendrils at the corners. The tendrils wrap around seaweed or stones to stop the cases floating away.

The case protects the pup growing inside it.

1 **⌃ Inside an egg case there is a tiny shark pup and white** yolk.

2 **≪ At three months, the shark pup's tail has grown longer.**

3

≫ After seven to ten months the swell shark pup is ready to hatch.

4

⌄ An adult swell shark can grow up to one metre long.

The story of a chicken

A hen is a female chicken. A male chicken is called a rooster or a cockerel. A chick is a baby chicken.

« When a rooster wants to mate, he crows loudly.

A hen's eggs will only grow into chicks if she has already mated with a rooster. The hen starts to lay her eggs a day after mating.

>> When the hen has laid her eggs she sits on them to keep them warm. This is called brooding.

<< Inside the egg, the chick gets food from the yellow yolk and the clear albumen.

The eggs hatch

After growing for about three weeks, the young chicks are ready to break out of their eggs.

« The chick chips a hole all around the shell.

Each chick has a sharp point on their top beak, called an egg-tooth. The chick uses its egg-tooth to crack a hole in the shell and push its way out.

4

« The newly hatched chick cheeps loudly. It is tired and its feathers are wet.

⌄ Once their feathers have dried, chicks become fluffy.

5

Life as a chick

The hen looks after her newly hatched chicks. She keeps them warm under her wings.

⌄ Newly hatched chicks stay close to their mother.

>> The chicks grow red, fleshy combs on top of their heads. The combs help them to keep cool.

v Chicks and chickens like to scratch in the dirt for tasty worms or bugs to eat.

The chicks grow into adults in just a few months. Glossy feathers grow in place of the soft, fluffy feathers. Soon the young hens will start to lay eggs.

The story of a kangaroo

Kangaroos are **mammals**. Mammals have fur and give birth to babies, which they feed with milk.

>> **When male kangaroos, called jacks, want to mate with females, they fight with one another.**

Kangaroos belong to a group of mammals called **marsupials**. A marsupial mother has a special pouch. She keeps the baby in her pouch while it grows bigger.

⌃ A baby kangaroo is called a joey. When it is born, it is little bigger than a fingernail.

≫ Kangaroos have long, strong legs, perfect for jumping across Australia's wide grasslands.

New life begins

When a male and female kangaroo mate, the male fertilizes a tiny egg inside the female's body.

⩒ Before a female gives birth, she cleans her pouch and licks a path across her belly.

The joey grows inside the female's body for nearly five weeks. As soon as the joey is born, it grips its mother's fur and pulls itself up her body to her pouch.

>> The arrow shows the joey's journey. This is the path the mother licked.

⌃ Inside the pouch, the joey finds its mother's nipple.

Ready, steady, grow!

Inside the pouch, a joey feeds, sleeps and grows. It is a cosy place for a young animal.

⌃ The mother cleans her joey and the pouch by licking them with her long tongue.

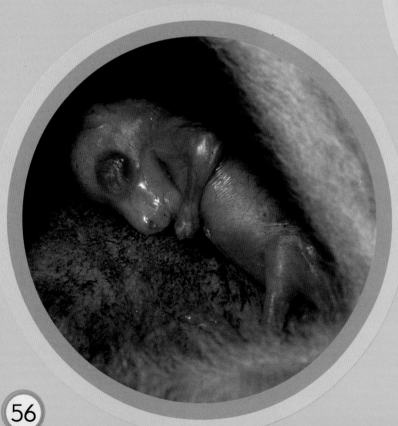

≪ For the first few months, the joey slowly grows bigger.

A joey watches what goes on around it.

The joey stays attached to its mother's nipple for about 10 weeks. It is nearly five months old before it can open its eyes. Then it pushes its head out and looks around.

Leaving the pouch

When it is about six months old, the joey leaves the pouch for the first time.

Joeys return to the pouch for milk or to sleep. When the joey is about eight months old, the mother stops it climbing into her pouch. A new joey is growing there now.

« When a joey is scared, it stays safe in its mother's pouch.

∨ When they are 18 to 24 months old, kangaroos are ready to mate.

« Although this joey is too big to get into the pouch, it still feeds on its mother's milk.

Glossary

albumen The white part inside an egg.

amphibian An animal that spends the first part of its life cycle in the water, and the second part mostly on land.

brooding When a hen sits on her eggs to keep them warm.

colony A group of animals that live together.

comb The soft, red skin on top of a chicken's head.

courtship When males and females are planning to mate.

fertilize When a special male cell joins with a female's egg so it can grow into a new living thing.

fin Part of a fish's body that is used to swim.

gill Part of a fish or tadpole's body used to breathe underwater.

hibernate To spend the winter months in a kind of deep sleep.

insect A small animal with six legs. Butterflies are insects.

mammal An animal that has fur and feeds its young with milk.

marsupial A type of mammal that gives birth to very small young. Some marsupials keep their young safe in a pouch.

mate When a male and female come together and a new life starts to grow.

migration A long journey made by an animal.

moulting When an animal sheds, or gets rid of, its old skin or feathers.

placenta Part of an animal's egg joins with the mother's body to create a placenta. Food is passed to the growing animal through the placenta.

poisonous Harmful to eat.

pupa The life stage during which a caterpillar changes into an adult butterfly.

scales Hard little pieces of skin that cover a fish's body.

tadpole When a young frog hatches from its egg and lives all the time in water.

yolk Part of an egg that provides food for a growing animal.

Index

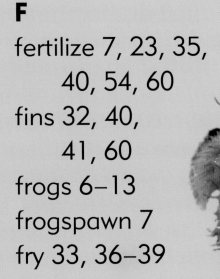

Picture credits